A Kid's Guide to Japan

Curious Kids Press • Palm Springs, CA
www.curiouskidspress.com

A WORD TO PARENTS

CURIOUS KIDS PRESS is passionate about helping young readers expand and enhance their understanding about countries and cultures around the world. While actual real-world experiences with other countries and cultures may have the most profound positive effect on children and pre-teens, we understand such experiences are not always possible. That's why our two series of books — "A Kid's Guide to . . ." (for ages 9-12) and "Let's Visit . . ." (for ages 6-8) — are designed to bridge that gap and help young readers explore the wonderful world of diversity in everything from food and holidays to geography and traditions. We hope your young explorers enjoy this adventure into the awesome country of Japan.

On the Cover: An illustrator's conception of a Japanese Koi, the national fish of Japan.

Publisher: Curious Kids Press, Palm Springs, CA 92264.
Designed by: Michael Owens
Editor: Sterling Moss
Copy Editor: Janice Ross

Copyright © 2019 by Curious Kids Press. All rights reserved. Except that any text portion of this book may be reproduced – mechanically, electronically, by hand or any other means you can think of – by any kid, anywhere, any time. For more information: info@curiouskidspress.com or 760-992-5962.

Table of Contents

Chapter 1
Welcome to Japan.................................... 4
Your Passport to Japan............................. 5
Where in the World Is Japan....................... 6
A Brief History of Japan............................ 8
Cool Facts About Japan............................. 10

Chapter 2
People, Customs, and Traditions....................13

Chapter 3
Landmarks and Attractions......................... 25

Chapter 4
The Animals of Japan................................ 35

Glossary 42
For Parents and Teachers........................... 46

Chapter 1

Welcome to Japan

WHAT IS JAPAN LIKE? The short answer to that question is "it depends."

Japan can be divided into eight major regions. Each region has its own **dialect**, customs, traditional culture, and even favorite food and weather.

For example, in the Kanto region, you might go hiking or skiing in the Alps or visit a fascinating castle in Matsumoto. (*See page 28*). On the other hand, in Okinawa, which is **subtropical,** you can enjoy the beach. There is also a small island called Taketomi where there are no cars, only bicycles.

If you have ever taken karate lessons, eaten sushi, or played just about any video game, then you already know a little bit about Japan. But there is so much more to discover about Japan.

So, come along, as we explore this awesome country – one of the safest and friendliest countries in the world.

Your Passport to Japan

Official Name: Japan (in Japanese Nihon or Nippon).
Country Area (Size): 145,914 sq. mi. (377,915 sq. km).
Population: 126,168,156 (as of 2018); (11th largest; slightly smaller than Mexico).
Official Languages: Japanese.
Money: Japanese Yen.
Religion: Mostly Buddhists or Shintoists.
National Day: May 17 (Constitution Day).

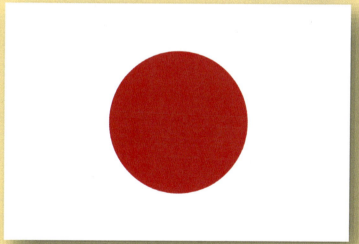

THE NATIONAL FLAG OF JAPAN is white with a large red disk in the center. The disk represents (or stands for) the sun without rays.

Did You Know? Although there are four main islands of Japan, there are also more than 6,000 smaller islands, too. But people live on only about 400 of them.

Where in the World Is Japan?

JAPAN IS LOCATED in Eastern Asia between the North Pacific Ocean and the Sea of Japan. It consists of four main islands and more than 6,000 smaller islands. The largest island – Honshu – is the seventh largest island in the world.

Japan's Four Largest Islands

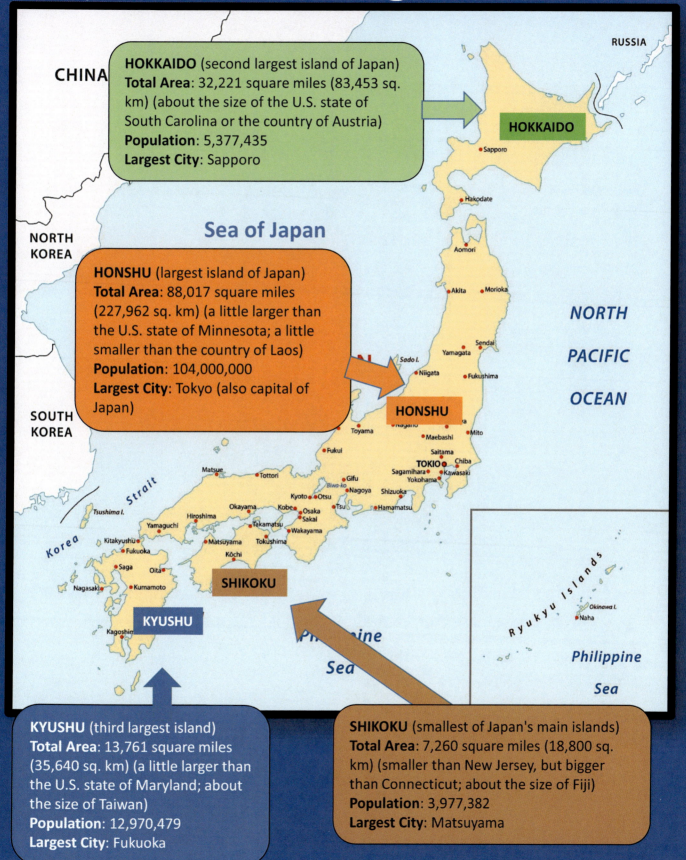

A Brief History of Japan

30,000 B.C.: People start coming into the islands of Japan.

660 B.C.: Jimmu, the **mythical** founder of Japan and the country's first emperor, comes to power.

Emperor Jimmu, the legendary first emperor of Japan.

794: Japan's imperial court is relocated from Nara, the country's first capital, to Kyoto. Kyoto remains the capital for the next 1,000 years.

1185: The first shōgun, or military dictator, comes to power in Japan. Shōguns rule the country for the next 700 years.

1633: The shōgun closes Japan to foreigners. He also prevents Japanese from leaving the country. The policy is known as "locked country."

1868: The shogun is overthrown and emperors return.

1869: The capital of Japan moves from Kyoto to Tokyo.

1914-1917: Japan fights on the side of the allies (Britain, France, Belgium, Russia, and the USA) during World War I.

1939-1945: Japan sides with the Axis powers (Germany, Italy) during World War II.

1941: Japan attacks Pearl Harbor in Hawaii. The United States enters World War II.

1945: The United States drops an atomic bomb on the cities of Hiroshima and Nagasaki. Soon afterwards, Japan surrenders.

1951: Japan becomes a **parliamentary democracy.**

The only structure left standing in the area where the first atomic bomb exploded now serves as an expression of world peace. Today, the structure is known as the Hiroshima Peace Memorial.

Cool Facts About Japan

In Japanese, the name "Japan" is Nihon (or Nippon). It means "Land of the Rising Sun."

In 2019, Crown Prince Naruhito became the 126th emperor of Japan. He is considered to be a direct **descendant** of the first emperor of Japan more than 2,500 years ago. Today, Japan is the only country in the world with a reigning emperor.

The emperor of Japan is the symbol of the nation. But has little political power. The country is a **constitutional monarchy**.

The Japanese writing system is made up of more than 60,000 kanji. Kanji are Chinese characters that are used in the Japanese writing system.

Most Japanese people have a general knowledge of about 3,000 to 4,000 kanji. Most books and newspapers use only about 1,850 kanji. High school students are expected to master those 1,850 kanji.

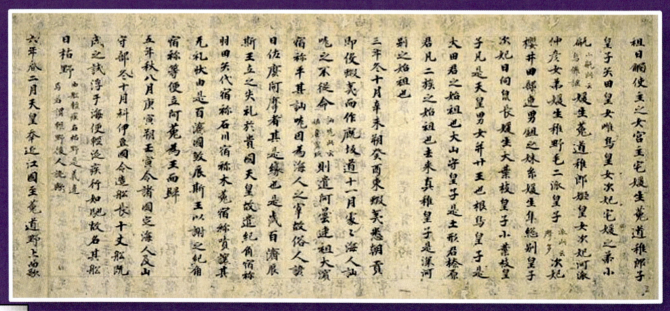

Quick Quiz

Only one of the following statements is false. Which one?

(a) The national symbol of Japan is the Bengal Tiger.

(b) Japan has more McDonald's restaurants than any other country in the world except the U.S.

(c) Taking a nap during the work day in Japan is a sign of a hard worker.

(**Answer:** (a) The Bengal Tiger is the national symbol of India.)

Strange But True

Christmas is not a religious holiday in Japan. But it is still celebrated with decorated trees, holiday shopping, and an annual Christmas parade including an appearance by Santa Claus. There is also another Christmas tradition in Japan: Eating Kentucky Fried Chicken on Christmas Eve.

Nice to Meet You

In the United States and other countries, when two people meet, they usually shake hands.

In Japan, when two people meet they usually bow. The lowest bow shows the greatest respect.

Cool Facts About Japan, cont.

SAVE ME A SEAT!

At outdoor festivals or special events in parks, it is customary for people to reserve a seating area. They do this by putting down a blue plastic mat where they want to sit. Once a mat is put down, the spot is considered taken. There's no need to stay with the mat. No one would move it or try to sit on it.

Haiku Poetry

Haiku poetry was invented in Japan. It is the shortest type of poem. There are only three lines in a Haiku poem. The lines do not rhyme.

The first line has five syllables; the second line has seven syllables; and the third line has five syllables. (A syllable is part of a word that is pronounced as a unit. The word introduction has four syllables.)

Read the Haiku poem abut Japan on the left of this box. Then try writing your own Haiku.

Thousands of islands
Old and new culture abounds
Did you guess? Japan.

Video Games

A Japanese video game designer created Nintendo's Pokémon. He came up with the idea when he imagined bugs crawling back and forth. (As a kid, he collected bugs.) The word Pokémon is short for the original Japanese title Pocket Monsters.

Chapter 2

People, Customs, And Traditions
Cherry Blossom Festival

EVERY SPRING THROUGHOUT JAPAN, there is a special festival called *hanami*. The word hanami means "viewing flowers." During the hanami festival, people everywhere go out to a park to view or see the cherry blossoms (*sakura*).

In many ways, the hanami festival is like a picnic. People bring food and drink. It's a special time of year in Japan.

Geisha

THE GEISHA has been an important part of Japanese culture for more than 1,500 years. Years ago, there were about 80,000 geishas in Japan. Today, there are only about 1,000.

Geisha are women who have special training in singing, dancing, and playing the samisen (a lute-like instrument). That's not surprising because the word geisha in Japanese means "art person" or "entertainer." (*gei* = art; *sha* = person)

Geisha

Why Is a Geisha's Face Painted White?

A geisha is probably best known for her kimono and her white-painted face. But did you know why a geisha's face is white? Years ago, homes in Japan were lit by candlelight, not electricity. Geishas would paint their faces white to help them stand out from other people attending a party.

7 Fun Facts about GEISHAS

1. It takes at least 12 months of training before a young woman can become a geisha.
2. Geishas live together in a house called an okiya.
3. During training, a geisha is not allowed to use a cell phone or email.
4. A geisha is not allowed to get married as long as she is working as a geisha.
5. Geishas learn to perform a dance called the shimai. Each gesture or movement in the dance has a special meaning.
6. To be a geisha, a young woman cannot be taller than 5 ft, 3 in. (1.6 m) tall.
7. A geisha's kimono and wig can weigh as much as 22 lbs. (10 kg). A kimono can cost as much as $10,000.

Sitting Seiza on Tatami Floors

EVERYWHERE YOU GO in Japan – houses, temples, restaurants – you're sure to find tatami. What's a tatami? A tatami is a type of floor. In a tatami room, you sit on thin mats on the floor.

The formal or polite way to sit on Japanese tatami floors is called seiza. The word means "proper sitting."

To sit seiza, place your knees on the floor and rest your behind on the top of your feet. The tops of your feet should be flat on the floor.

Seiza is a requirement at formal Japanese ceremonies such as funerals. It's also a requirement of most Japanese martial arts. Many people find it hard to sit seiza for very long.

The judo practitioners (above) are sitting seiza.

Sumo Wrestling

SUMO WRESTLING is Japan's national sport, even though baseball is the most popular sport in Japan. The first sumo wrestling match was nearly two thousand years ago.

Today's sumo wrestlers **dedicate** their lives to the sport. Sumo wrestlers live, train, and sleep together in what's called a stable. They are expected to be dignified and honorable at all times.

A boy as young as 15 years old can join a stable with the hope of becoming a sumo wrestler or maybe even a grand champion, known as a *Yokozuna*.

Each year there are six sumo tournaments throughout the country. Each one lasts 15 days. Before a wrestling match, sumo wrestlers toss salt into the ring. They believe the salt will **purify** the ring and drive out bad spirits.

An Imaginary Interview with a SUMO WRESTLER

If you could ask a sumo wrestler a question, what would it be?

How much do you weigh?

Around 350 pounds. That's the average weight of most sumo wrestlers.

How much do you eat every day?

Sumo wrestlers eat about 10,000 calories per day.

Why do you wear your hair in a knot on top of your head?

You might call it a man-bun. In Japan it's called a topknot or chonmage. It is an important symbol of honor. Special barbers are hired to style our hair. When a sumo wrestler retires, the chonmage is cut off.

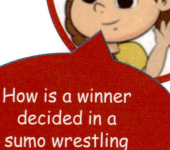

How is a winner decided in a sumo wrestling match?

The first wrestler to be pushed out of the ring or to touch the ring with anything but the soles of his feet loses.

Can a woman be a professional sumo wrestler?

No. In fact, a woman is not even allowed to enter the sumo ring.

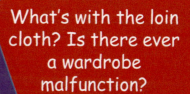

What's with the loin cloth? Is there ever a wardrobe malfunction?

The loin cloth is a 30-foot long piece of cotton (for training) or silk (for tournaments) wrapped tightly around the wrestler's body. If it comes off during a match, the wrestler loses – and is probably pretty embarrassed

The Samurai: Japanese Warriors

FOR MORE THAN 700 years, men known as **samurai** were some of the most important men in all of Japan. They were both warriors as well as part of the ruling class of Japanese society.

As warriors, the samurai were excellent fighters. Their main weapon was a sharp sword with a slight curve to it. The samurai's sword was his most prized possession. Samurai warriors even named their swords. They believed their swords carried their warrior spirit.

As part of the ruling class, the samurai dominated Japanese government and society. They promised complete loyalty to shoguns (or military dictators).

Samurai followed a strict code of conduct, called *bushido*. There were strict rules for almost every part of everyday life. They were expected to be fiercely loyal to honor, duty, and service. Those three qualities are important in Japanese culture today.

In 1868, **feudalism** in Japan came to an end. That also marked the end of the samurai. Today, there are no samurai. Yet, the descendants of samurai in Japan are well respected.

> **Fun Fact**
> Some women were also samurai. They received the same training in martial arts as the men. They also took part in combat.

> **Fun Fact**
> The term "samurai" comes from the Japanese word *saburau*, meaning "to serve" or "those who serve."

Armored samurai with sword and dagger (1860)

People, Customs and Traditions, cont.

The Martial Arts Karate, Judo, and Aikido

THERE ARE MANY DIFFERENT KINDS of martial arts. But they all have one thing in common. They are a form of self-defense.

People who practice the martial arts say they do much more. They can help improve self-confidence or concentration. They also help improve balance, strength, and stamina.

Three of the most common styles of Japanese martial arts are karate, judo, and aikido. Here is a brief look at each one.

KARATE is primarily a *striking* martial art. The name comes from the two Japanese words: *kara*, meaning "empty" and *te*, meaning "hand." The full name of Karate is "Karate-do" which means "the way of the empty hand" in English.

People who practice karate use all parts of their body (hands, feet, elbows, fingers, etc.) to kick, punch, chop, butt, and more, all as a method of self-defense.

But in karate, it is not size and strength alone that win. Speed and knowledge are often the deciding factors in who will emerge victorious in physical combat.

In the United States, the first karate school (or *dojo*) was opened in Phoenix, Arizona, in 1945. Today, there are many different karate schools throughout the world, and many different styles of karate practiced by both kids and adults alike.

JUDO got its start in Japan in 1882. It was created as a physical, mental, and moral exercise, as well as a method of self-defense. The objective of judo is to either throw or take down an opponent to the ground, almost always without striking in blows. In fact, the term judo translates as "the gentle way."

A judo practitioner is called a judoka. Judo concentrates primarily on defensive maneuvers, utilizing close-range grappling and throwing techniques to push or pull an opponent off-balance and bring him or her to the ground.

Judo became an Olympic sport in the 1960s.

AIKIDO is a martial art that is peaceful in nature. It was founded during the 1920's and 30's in Japan.

It emphasizes "holds" instead of strikes. It teaches practitioners how to use an opponent's own aggression against him or her. For example, if an attacker tries to throw a punch, the aikido practitioner might step aside, grab the wrist of the attacker, and use the attacker's own momentum to throw him off balance.

In Aikido, a practitioner learns to protect himself or herself without seriously harming the attacker. In fact, the word aikido translates as "the way of **harmonious** (or peaceful) spirit."

People, Customs, and Traditions, cont.

Karaoke: A Japanese Invention

THERE IS A POPULAR singing activity throughout the world. It's known as karaoke and it got its start in – you guessed it – Japan in 1969.

Karaoke is a form of musical entertainment. A special device plays the instrumental version of popular songs. The lyrics (or words) to the song are displayed on a video screen, often with a moving color symbol over each word as the words are sung, usually by an amateur singer.

Karaoke first became popular when there was a strike among orchestra players. The name karaoke comes from "*kara okesutura*," which means "empty orchestra." "Kara okesutura" was later shortened to karaoke.

Today, karaoke machines can turn your own backyard into an exciting musical scene.

Did You Know?

The very first set of emoji was invented by a young Japanese man in 1999.

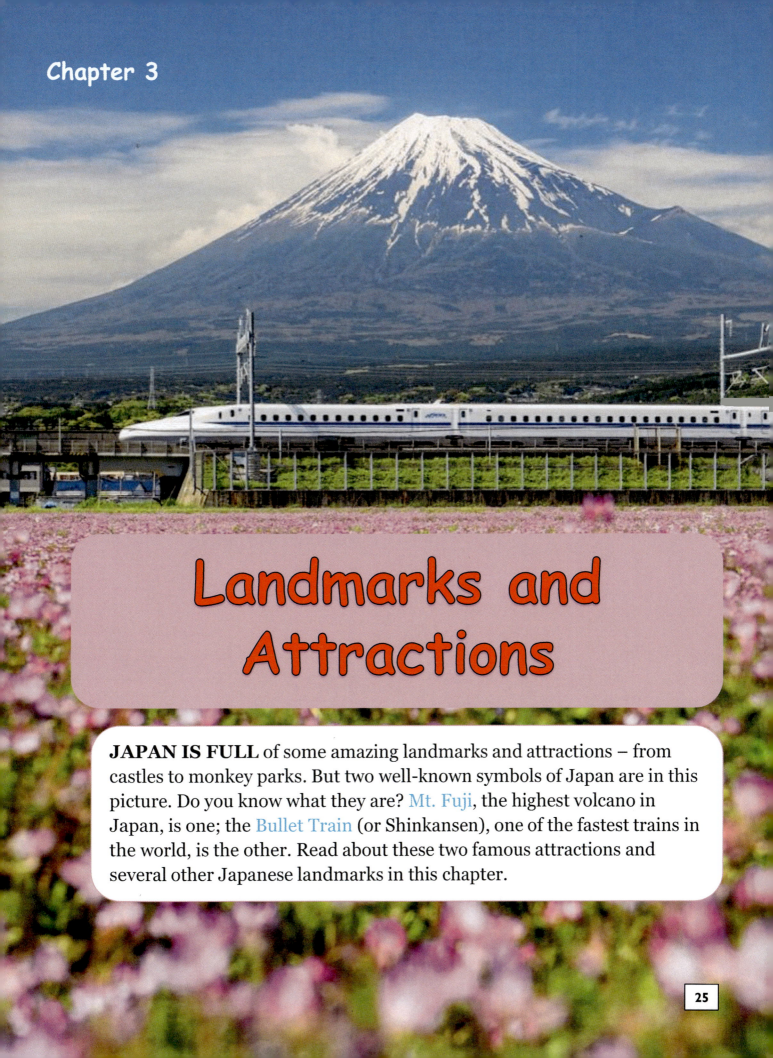

Chapter 3

Landmarks and Attractions

JAPAN IS FULL of some amazing landmarks and attractions – from castles to monkey parks. But two well-known symbols of Japan are in this picture. Do you know what they are? Mt. Fuji, the highest volcano in Japan, is one; the Bullet Train (or Shinkansen), one of the fastest trains in the world, is the other. Read about these two famous attractions and several other Japanese landmarks in this chapter.

Landmarks and Attractions, cont.

The Bullet Train

IT'S CALLED THE BULLET TRAIN. And one look at the front of the train tells you why.

The bullet train is actually a series of trains that travel throughout Japan with names like Strong Wind or Wings – perfect names for trains that can reach speeds of up to 200 mph (320 km/h). (That's about the speed of a commercial jet before it lifts off the runway.)

Japan's high-speed electric train was launched in 1964 just in time for the opening of the 1964 Summer Olympics in Tokyo. It was a big success. It cut travel time between Tokyo and Osaka from seven hours to four hours.

There was just one problem. It created a loud boom when it came out of a tunnel. The noise disturbed the neighborhoods and people complained.

A Japanese designer had an idea. He was a birdwatcher and had noticed how the kingfisher, a bird with a long narrow beak, would dive into water without creating much splash.

He wondered if the same principle or idea could reduce the noise from the train. Sure enough, it did.

And, so, the bullet train with the long sleek nose was born.

The Kingfisher

Mount Fuji

MOUNT FUJI is one of Japan's most famous sites. It is a stratovolcano that measures 12,389 ft. (3,776 m) high. That makes it the highest volcano in Japan. It is located about 60 miles (100 km) from Tokyo. The last time Mt. Fuji erupted was in 1707.

The first person to climb Mount Fuji was a Buddhist monk in 663. Today, it is the most climbed mountain in the world. More than 100,000 people climb Mt. Fuji every year.

Mount Fuji's climbing season lasts only two months long (between July and August). The weather is too bad the rest of year to attempt to climb it.

Landmarks and Attractions, cont.

The Matsumoto Castle

AT ONE TIME, there were more than 5,000 castles in Japan. They were built primarily of wood. Over the years, many were destroyed. But, today, there are still more than 100 castles in Japan.

One of Japan's oldest castles is Matsumoto. It was built around 1593. Inside, you will find steep stairs, low ceilings, and narrow windows once used by archers (a person who uses a bow and arrow) and gunmen.

Matsumoto Castle is also known as Crow Castle because of its black exterior. The main tower of the castle is five-tiered. But there are six floors. One floor is hidden halfway up the building.

During the day, costumed ninja and samurai roam the grounds of the Matsumoto Castle, entertaining kids and posing for photographs.

Skytree Tower

It's taller than the **Eiffel Tower** in Paris, France. That tower is only 1,063 ft. (324 m) tall.

It's taller than the **Stratosphere Tower** in Las Vegas, Nevada. That tower is only 1,149 ft. (350.2 m) tall.

FOR A GREAT VIEW of Tokyo, take a trip to the top of the tallest tower in the world – the Skytree Tower in Tokyo. It stands 2,080 ft. (634 m) tall. On a clear day, you might even see Mt. Fuji about 60 miles (97 km) away!

But Skytree may soon lose its title as tallest tower. There is another tower under construction in Dubai, United Arab Republic. It is supposed to be 2,716.5 ft. (828 m) tall when completed.

Landmarks and Attractions, cont.

Nara Park

BOWING IN JAPAN is as important as shaking hands in countries in the West. People bow in Japan to say hello, good-bye, thank you, excuse me, and to express many others feelings.

But did you know that there is a place in Japan where some deer bow?

That place is Nara Park, a public park in the city of Nara, Japan. The park is home to more than 1,000 deer. Many have learned to bow when asking to be fed or asking for treats. (Their favorite treats are rice crackers that tourists can buy from vendors in the park.)

The wild but tame deer roam freely in the park, which was established in 1880. It is one of the oldest parks in Japan.

Tokyo
The Capital of Japan

TOKYO is one of the largest cities in the world. More than 38 million people live there. That's more than the entire population of Canada.

So, it should come as no surprise that the busiest intersection in the world is in Tokyo. (*See photo.*) Every time the traffic light changes, more than 2,500 people surge forward without anyone bumping into anyone else. Pretty amazing!

Why is this pedestrian crossing so busy? For one thing, it is located at a subway station that handles more than two million people every day, all going to work or shopping in the area.

Tokyo is home to the Shibuya Crossing, the busiest pedestrian crosswalk in the world.

ON SEPTEMBER 1, 1923, A TERRIBLE EARTHQUAKE struck Tokyo. It lasted more than four minutes and totally destroyed the city. It was followed by a 40-foot high **tsunami** and dozens of fires.

The earthquake was so strong it moved the 90-ton Great Buddha statue (above) two feet forward. The bronze statue was cast in 1252 and is the second largest buddha statue in Japan. It stands 43.8 ft (13 m) tall.

Tokyo 2020
The Summer Olympics

IN 1964, TOKYO BECAME the first Asian city to host the Summer Olympics. More than 50 years later, Tokyo once again hosted the Summer Olympics, scheduled for 2020 but delayed until 2021 because of the Covid-19 pandemic.

The **2020 Summer Olympic Games** saw some new events, including karate, sport climbing, surfing, and skateboarding. Baseball and softball returned after a thirteen-year absence.

The United States won the most medals (113), as well as the most gold medals (39). China finished second in both number of medals and gold medals.

The new stadium under construction in Tokyo

Quick Quiz
Which country in the world has hosted more Olympic Games than any other?
(a) United States
(b) Japan
(c) France
Find out on page 43.

Previous Olympics in Japan
The modern Olympic Games have been held in Japan four times.
1964 Summer Olympics, Tokyo
1972 Winter Olympics, Sapporo
1998 Winter Olympics, Nagano
2020 Summer Olympics, Tokyo

5 Fun Facts About School in Japan

1. By the time teenagers are fifteen years old, they are expected to know more than 1,000 different kanji characters. (Kanji is like an alphabet.)

2. Most Japanese schools do not employ janitors or custodians. The students clean their schools themselves.

3. The Japanese school year starts in April and ends in March. Winter break is from December 26 to around January 6.

4. Kids are required to go to six years of elementary school and three years of junior high school. Most also go to four years of high school.

5. One of the goals of the first three years of school is to help students learn good manners and develop character.

6. Japanese secondary schools rarely use substitute teachers. If a teacher is out sick, students are trusted to study quietly and independently by themselves throughout the day.

Chapter 4
The Animals of Japan

JAPAN HAS A WIDE VARIETY of animals. That shouldn't be surprising, because the country has both very cold regions in the north and very warm regions in the south. Here are four groups of animals found in Japan.

MAMMALS: About 130 species
The largest mammals in Japan are two different species of bears: the Ussuri brown bear (below) and the Asian black bear.

BIRDS: More than 600 species
The Japanese Green Pheasant is the National Bird of Japan.

REPTILES AND AMPHIBIANS: About 73 species of reptiles and 40 species of amphibians.
The Japanese giant salamander is one of the largest salamanders in the world.

INSECTS: *More than 300 butterfly and many other cicadas, crickets, and fireflies.*
The Japanese Giant Hornet is one of the largest hornets in the world. In fact, its Japanese name means "giant sparrow bee."

The Animals of Japan, cont.

Japanese Snow Monkeys

**SNOW MONKEYS
At-a-Glance**

Length (head and body): 20 in. (500 mm) high.

Weight: (female): 19 lb (11.3 kg); (male) 25 lb (11.3 kg).

Lifespan: 20 years in captivity.

Diet: Omnivorous (including plants, fruits, insects).

Other: They are very good swimmers.

IMAGINE LIVING in an area where the temperature is as low as -4 °F (-20 °C). That's colder than the average temperature in Anchorage, Alaska, in January.

Maybe that's why the Japanese macaque (or snow monkeys) have such a cute pink face. They live in the coldest part of Japan in regions where no other **primates** or other animals can survive. Brrr. It's cold!

The macaque copes with the cold weather, however, in one important way. The thickness of its coat increases as the temperature decreases each year.

The Japanese macaque are supposedly very smart. If one macaque learns something new, he or she can pass on that knowledge to other macaques.

For example, some snow monkeys wash sweet potato in the water. They use salty water because they prefer salty taste of the food.

Snow monkeys are playful creatures. They often make snowballs and roll them on the ground during the winter. Adult animals also participate in this type of game – even when it's freezing cold outside.

The Animals of Japan, cont.

JAPANESE KOI
The National Fish of Japan

**KOI
At-a-Glance**

Length: Up to 3 feet (90 centimeters). (That's the same as the height of an average three-year-old.

Lifespan: 50 years on average

Diet: Omnivorous

IMAGINE A FISH worth $1.8 million. Impossible? Ridiculous?

Well, in 2017, someone actually paid that much for a single koi fish. The koi won Grand Champion at the All Japan Koi show.

Koi may look like nothing more than fat goldfish. But they are only distant relatives. They both are descendants of the carp, a rather dull-looking fish that can be found all over the world.

Koi are called **ornamental** fish. That's because of their many bright colors, like ornaments on a Christmas tree. In Japan, koi are symbols of love, friendship, and good luck.

There are more than two dozen named varieties of koi, including the Shōwa Sanke and the Kōhaku below.

Shōwa Sanke: Black koi with red and white markings.

`Hanako,` a Japanese Koi that supposedly lived for 226 years (1751–1977)

Kōhaku: White-skinned koi with large red markings on top.

Did You Know?
Koi are pretty smart. They can be trained to eat from your hand.

The Animals of Japan, cont.

Red-crowned Crane

RED-CROWNED CRANE
At-a-Glance
Stands: 5 ft (1.5 m) tall

Wingspan: 8 ft (2.5 m)

Weight: 22 lb (9.9 kg)

Diet: Omnivorous (parsley, carrots, acorns, various other plants; meat of various kinds; carp and other fish).

Lifespan: Up to 60 years.

Threats: Habitat destruction as development encroaches on wetlands that these birds need for breeding and living.

In Japan, the red-crowned crane is known as tancho ("red mountain").

THE JAPANESE RED-CROWNED CRANE is the second rarest crane **species** in the world, after the whopping crane. There are fewer than 2,600 worldwide.

They are also the tallest of all flying birds. They can fly at speeds of 40 mph (km/h).

Cranes are **symbols** of love, happiness, and longevity. So, it's no surprise that the image of the red-crowned crane is everywhere in Japan – on clothes, dishes, art, money, and so much more. The official logo of Japan airlines features a red-crowned crane.

Booth male and female have distinctive red crowns and white and black markings on their wings and bodies.

Glossary

constitutional monarchy: A form of government in which a king or queen rules a country according to a constitution (or basic laws of the nation).

dedicate (*verb*): To commit to a goal or a way of life.

descendant (*noun*): Someone who is related to a person who lived in the past.

dialect (*noun*): A form of language that is spoken in a particular region.

feudalism (*noun*): A social system in which people worked and fought for nobles in return for land and protection.

mammal (*noun*): a warm-blooded animal (such as a dog, whale, or human being) with a backbone that feeds its young with milk produced by the mother.

mythical (*adjective*): Imaginary, fictitious, unreal; not existing in fact.

ornamental (*adjective*): Decorative.

parliamentary democracy: A system of government in which the head of the government (who typically holds the title prime minister) is chosen by the legislature, rather than the people.

possession (*noun*): Something that is owned.

purify (*verb*): To free from dirt or contamination.

species (*noun*): A variety, type, or kind.

subtropical (*adjective*): Of or pertaining to regions north or south of the tropics.

symbol (*noun*): Something that represents or stands for something else.

tsunami (*noun*): A huge, powerful sea wave often caused by an earthquake under the sea.

Explore the World

Find these books on Amazon.com
Preview them at curiouskidspress.com

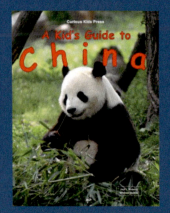
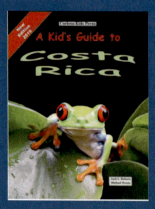
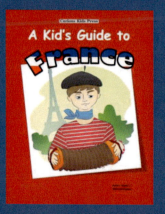
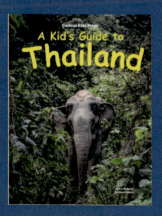
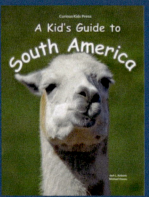

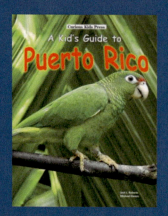
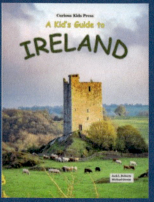
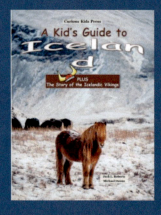
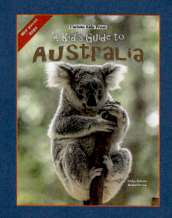
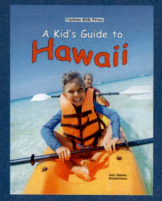
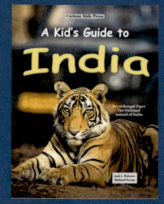

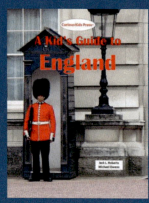
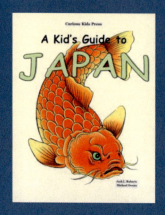
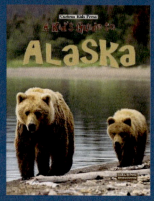

Curious Kids Press
www.curiouskidspress.com

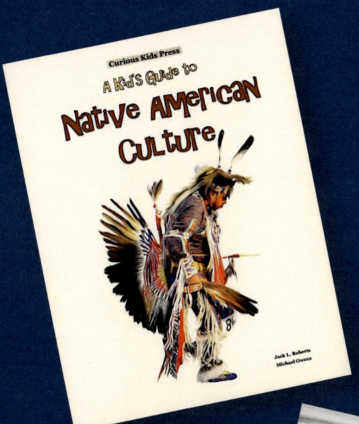

Two important new books for all young readers and their families.

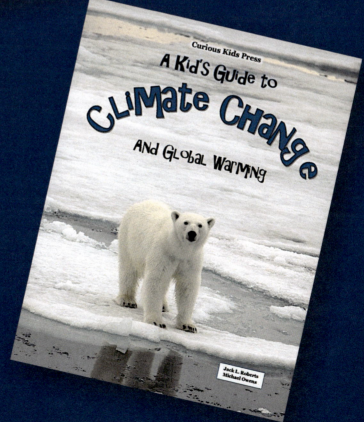

Available on amazon.com

A Kid's Guide to
Japan
For Parents and Teachers

About This Book

A Kid's Guide to . . . is an engaging, easy-to-read book series that provides an exciting adventure into fascinating countries and cultures around the world for young readers. Each book focuses on one country, continent, or U.S. territory or state, and includes colorful photographs, informational charts and graphs, and quirky and bizarre "Did You Know" facts, all designed to bring the country and its people to life. Designed primarily for recreational, high-interest reading, the informational text series is also a great resource for students to use to research geography topics or writing assignments.

About the Reading Level

A Kid's Guide to . . . is an informational text series designed for kids in grades 4 to 6, ages 9 to 12. For some young readers, the series will provide new reading challenges based on the vocabulary and sentence structure. For other readers, the series will review and reinforce reading skills already achieved. While for still other readers, the book will match their current skill level, regardless of age or grade level.

About the Authors

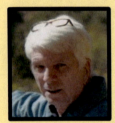

Jack L. Roberts began his career in educational publishing at Children's Television Workshop (now Sesame Workshop), where he was Senior Editor of The Sesame Street/Electric Company Reading Kits. Later, at Scholastic Inc., he was the founding editor of a high-interest/low-reading level magazine for middle school students. He also founded two technology magazines for teachers and administrators.

Roberts is the author of more than two dozen biographies and other nonfiction titles for young readers, published by Scholastic Inc., the Lerner Publishing Group, Teacher Created Materials, Benchmark Education, and others.. More recently, he was the co-founder of WordTeasers, an educational series of card decks designed to help kids of all ages improve their vocabulary through "conversation, not memorization."

Michael Owens is a noted jazz dance teacher, award-winning wildlife photographer, graphic arts designer, and devoted animal lover.

In 2017, Roberts and Owens launched Curious Kids Press (CKP), an educational publishing company focused on publishing high-interest, nonfiction books for young readers, primarily books about countries and cultures around the world. Currently, CKP has published two series of country books: "A Kid's Guide to..." (for ages 9-12 and "Let's Visit . . ." (for ages 6-8) — both designed to help young readers explore the wonderful world of diversity in everything from food and holidays to geography and traditions.

To Our Valued Customers

Curious Kids Press is passionate about creating fun-to-read books about countries and cultures around the world for young readers, and we work hard every day to create quality products.

All of our books are Print on Demand books. As a result, on rare occasions, you may find minor printing errors. If you feel you have not received a quality printed product, please send us a description and photo of the printing error along with your name and address and we will have a new copy sent to you free of charge. Contact us at: info@curiouskidspress.com

Made in the USA
Middletown, DE
16 March 2023